WASHINGTON, D.C.
PROTESTS

WASHINGTON, D.C.
PROTESTS

SCENES FROM **HOME RULE** TO
THE **CIVIL RIGHTS MOVEMENT**

MARK S. GREEK

Charleston   London

THE
History
PRESS

Published by The History Press
Charleston, SC 29403
www.historypress.net

First published 2009

Manufactured in the United States

ISBN 978.1.59629.786.9

Library of Congress Cataloging-in-Publication Data
Greek, Mark S.
Washington, D.C. protests : scenes from home rule to the civil rights movement / Mark
S. Greek.
p. cm.
ISBN 978-1-59629-786-9
1. Washington (D.C.)--Politics and government--20th century--Pictorial works.
2. Washington (D.C.)--Social conditions--20th century--Pictorial works. 3. Home
rule--Washington (D.C.)--History--20th century--Pictorial works. 4. Protest
movements--Washington (D.C.)--History--20th century--Pictorial works. 5. Civil rights
movements--Washington (D.C.)--History--20th century--Pictorial works. 6. Civil rights
demonstrations--Washington (D.C.)--History--20th century--Pictorial works. I. Title.
F195.G74 2009
975.3'04--dc22
2009037772

For Eva Cate

Contents

FOREWORD

Mark Greek has compiled a fabulous collection of photos that brilliantly tell the story of D.C.'s journey to become part of America. It is difficult for some to imagine living in the nation's capital and being denied the rights that every other American takes for granted. Yet it was not until 1964 that D.C. citizens were even allowed to vote in presidential elections. This alone should make people irate and ashamed of such a broken system. Even today, 570,000 citizens do not have a voting representative in the U.S. House or U.S. Senate. As Senator Edward M. Kennedy once said in analyzing the terrible situation and why it was so difficult to convince Congress to grant suffrage to the District, D.C. suffers from being "too urban, too liberal, too Democratic [in party affiliation] and too black." Just look at the faces of District residents in Rebecca Kingsley's film, *The Last Colony*. There is intensity and a deep sense of purpose in those who are denied their rights.

The rest of the country does not know our history or our struggle. D.C. is more than a collection of buildings and monuments. Real people live here, and for far too long they have been and continue to be treated as second-class citizens. The pictures in this book chronicle every stage of this last chapter of the American civil rights story.

There are great images of legendary local and national figures: Joe Rauh, Lyndon Baines Johnson, Abe Fortas, Cliff Alexander, Thurgood Marshall, Walter Washington and Sterling Tucker. The wonderful cartoons of Clifford Berryman also grace this indispensable book. Best of all, D.C. citizens, not famous but all passionate about exposing our nation's dirty little secret, are shown in all their glory. This fight is not over. D.C. statehood is the ultimate goal that we hope to achieve in our lifetime. Look at these images and be inspired to work for our rights. From the civil rights movement to the struggle for local suffrage, Washingtonians have a strong history of making positive change through protest. D.C. owes a huge thank-you to Mark Greek for this memorable, important and essential piece of work.

Mark Plotkin
WTOP Political Commentator and Analyst

ACKNOWLEDGEMENTS

All images contained within this volume are from the collections of the D.C. Public Library's Washingtoniana Division. The majority of the images come from the *Washington Star* collection and are copyrighted to the *Washington Post*; they are reprinted here with the permission of the D.C. Public Library. Additional images were selected from the division's D.C. Community Archives and the Historical Image Collection. Since 1905, Washingtoniana's mission has been to collect and preserve the history of Washington, D.C., and its people. Today the collection consists of over 1,200 linear feet of archival collections, more than twenty-five thousand books, over eight thousand maps, millions of vertical files and clippings, newspapers, periodicals, government documents and 1.2 million photographs. The collection is considered to be the largest "local history" collection at any public library in the United States.

I came to Washingtoniana in 2002, and since that time the main focus of my job has been to preserve and increase access to the division's image collections. To date, I have processed over 400,000 images, and with the creation of several in-house databases, searching the collections has become much easier. We have established a flickr website account to highlight some images in our collection and are currently developing a digital archive, which we hope to launch in early to mid-2010.

I am eternally thankful to my fellow staff members and Karen Blackman-Mills, head of Special Collections, for all their assistance in the creation of this book. A special thanks to my wife Ashley, whose support and encouragement are truly responsible for this work. Lastly, I am greatly indebted to those who donated their images to the collections of Washingtoniana over the past one hundred years; without their generous gifts this work truly would never have been able to happen. And to those who still have images and ephemera in their attics and basements, I encourage you to find a suitable repository for them and not simply toss them in the trash. As Katherine Patten, first curator of Washingtoniana, once said, "The gift of a book, a photograph or a pamphlet to the collection is a gift to the city as a whole."

INTRODUCTION

For over two hundred years, District of Columbia residents have given to this country. They have given their sons and daughters in times of war, paid their taxes and supported their government. But despite this devotion, this country has not equally given to them. Since the city's establishment in 1801, D.C. citizens have, in one form or another, been denied a basic constitutional right: the right to vote. D.C.'s struggle to gain a vote languished in obscurity until it found kinship with the civil rights movement. A shared disenfranchisement by the federal government brought them together, and with common cause they continue to march forward toward a seemingly elusive goal.

The question of where to locate the nation's capital was first raised in 1783, and several locations were proposed, but southern states refused to accept a capital in the North, while northern states refused to accept a capital in the South. The debate over the location of the city was again raised at the 1787 Constitutional Convention. Article I, Section 8, of the United States Constitution granted Congress power over a federal district; however, it failed to choose a suitable location. On July 16, 1790, Congress finally reached a compromise and a site on the Potomac River near Georgetown, Maryland, was chosen. The Residence Act provided for a permanent capital city of no more than one hundred square miles to be selected by President George Washington and charged him with selecting a three-member Board of Commissioners to oversee its construction. With this act, the city of Washington was created, and the fight for home rule and voting rights was born.

Washington selected and surveyed the site, which included parts of the cities of Georgetown, Maryland, and Alexandria, Virginia. James Madison and John Adams each believed that the new federal city would grant its citizens a local government, and the residents of this area believed this as well. They continued to vote in Maryland and Virginia elections and enjoyed representation in the state legislatures. The states also continued to write laws and fund the construction of the new city. However, when the charter was finally established, it lacked the total autonomous control that Madison and Adams envisioned.

In 1801, the Organic Act officially organized the new federal district and placed the entire territory, including the cities of Georgetown and Alexandria, under the exclusive control of Congress. The following year, the city of Washington was incorporated, with a charter calling for a local government consisting of an appointed mayor and an elected six-member council. In 1820, the charter was amended to allow for an elected mayor. During this period, the local governments operated independently of each other, often causing conflicting statutes and laws. Although the citizens of this new federal district retained their independent local government, they replaced their state representation with a federal presence of which they had no control.

In essence, the Organic Act of 1801 stripped the citizens of the new federal district of their basic right to representation and congressional voting rights. Since that time, this distinction has been reserved for minorities, felons and traitors. The Fifteenth and Nineteenth constitutional amendments granted voting rights to minorities; however, the citizens of the District would continue without a national voice at the ballot box for the next 159 years.

During these early years of the city's history, Congress took a laissez faire approach to dealing with city affairs. However, that all changed with the election of President Andrew Jackson and the pro-Jackson Congress. Congress began intervening in local affairs, mainly disputes over the financing of capital projects. In 1840, these disputes became more political when the citizens of Washington elected a member of the anti-Jackson Whig Party as mayor. Two weeks after the election, Congress submitted legislation that would have removed the city's elected government. This measure failed but illustrated the growing rift between the federal and local sides of the District.

In 1846, Virginia successfully petitioned Congress for the return of its land, including the city of Alexandria. The remaining jurisdictions continued to develop a complicated, piecemeal local government. Each area retained separate municipal authority, but constant struggles with overlapping authorities, such as the Metropolitan Police Department, continued to impede progress. Following the Civil War, the city lacked basic sanitation and adequate roads, a problem that had some members of Congress proposing moving the capital elsewhere.

In order to fix the infrastructure problems and make the city's government operate more effectively, and only having a non-voting local population to oppose it, Congress passed the Organic Act of 1871. The new act combined the cities of Washington and Georgetown under one municipality, officially named the District of Columbia. Gone was the elected government. It was replaced with a Board of Public Works, and in 1873, President Ulysses Grant appointed Alexander Shepherd to the new post of governor. That year, Shepherd spent $20 million on public works, which modernized the city but also left it bankrupt. In 1874, Congress abolished the territorial government in favor of direct rule.

The office of governor was replaced by a three-member Board of Commissioners, two members to be appointed by the president after approval by the Senate, while the third member was selected from the Army Corps of Engineers. For nearly a century, this form of government controlled the District of Columbia. In the years following World War II, six different pieces of legislation were introduced to give the citizens of D.C. some form of home rule; each failed. The congressional logjam that prevented any home rule legislation was finally broken by the civil rights movement and the support of Presidents Dwight Eisenhower, John Kennedy and Lyndon Johnson.

By the 1950s, D.C. had become a black majority city, and its fate became intertwined with that of the struggles of the civil rights movement. As demonstrators descended on the capital, the citizens of D.C. found common ground with those who had also been disenfranchised by their government. Working with momentum created by the civil rights movement, in 1960 Eisenhower pushed for and Congress ratified the Twenty-third Amendment to the Constitution, which granted residents of the District of Columbia the right to vote in presidential elections.

In 1967, Johnson was able get Congress to do away with the three-commissioner form of government, stating that "for much too long this Nation has tolerated in the District of Columbia conditions that our ancestors fought a revolution to eliminate." It was replaced with a mayor-commissioner and nine-member city council appointed by the president. During this same period, the city gained an elected school board, and for the first time in nearly one hundred years the voice of local suffrage was heard again.

Basic home rule was granted to the citizens of the District of Columbia in 1973 with the enacting of the District of Columbia Home Rule Act, which provided for a mayor and a thirteen-member city council. This new local government, still in effect today, has the ability to pass local laws and ordinances. However, pursuant to the Home Rule Act, all legislation passed by the mayor and council, including the budget, remains subject to the approval of Congress.

The year 1968 saw the formation of the D.C. Statehood Committee, which remains ever vigilant in its quest to see New Columbia join the union as the fifty-first state. The D.C. Election Act was passed in 1970, giving the District a non-voting delegate to the House of Representatives. In the 1980s, Walter Fauntroy led the charge for a constitutional amendment to give the city voting power in the Senate and House of Representatives, but this measure was doomed when only sixteen out of the needed thirty-eight states ratified the measure. Over the past two decades, small steps have been gained, but congressional voting rights have still eluded the citizens of the District of Columbia.

Washingtonians have continued to fight for those rights afforded them by the U.S. Constitution. The United Nations Human Rights Committee has found that the District of Columbia's lack of voting representation in Congress violates the International Covenant on Civil and Political Rights, a treaty ratified by more than 160 countries, including the United States. Over the past few decades, District residents have vigorously fought for a variety of civil and political rights issues. Although victories have been won and residents now enjoy more freedoms than those of the previous generations, many challenges still remain. The questions now are who will lead the charge into the next battle and how long will Washingtonians have to continue to wait for complete home rule and full voting rights in Congress?

THE EARLY DAYS OF THE HOME RULE MOVEMENT

In the early days of Washington, it is very doubtful that many citizens complained about their lack of representation. After all, they had an elected city council, and in 1820, residents were given the authority to elect their own mayor. But as the federal government began to exert more influence over the day-to-day lives of citizens, Washingtonians began to realize their true lack of influence in the halls of Congress. By the 1860s, Washington was no longer a sleepy little town. And with a population of over 120,000, and growing, it was becoming clear that the old way of doing things no longer worked. Without a national voice, Washingtonians were helpless and could not avoid the 1871 government takeover. Washingtonians actively pushed for the reinstatement of home rule but made little progress. By 1920, only felons, traitors, the insane and Washingtonians lacked the right to vote. By organizing in parlors and taking to the streets, D.C. residents began to express their desire for home rule. Within twenty years, they had the attention of Congress; however, most proposed legislations died in committee. In 1948, the first bill that provided for local self-government reached the floor of the House of Representatives. It was proposed by Congressman James Auchincloss of New Jersey, and from the moment the debate opened it was staunchly opposed by Congressman Oren Harris of Ohio. He demanded that the entire ninety-page document be read word for word. This filibuster technique caused an impatient majority to shelve the bill. So it was for the home rule movement, which took no steps forward until Lyndon Johnson became president.

Above: At the 1913 Women's Suffrage March, sponsored by the National American Women Suffrage Association, some Washingtonians took advantage of the situation to call attention to the fact that residents of the nation's capital had been without a national voice for over one hundred years.

Left: Even after the passage of the Nineteenth Amendment to the Constitution in 1920, which granted women the right to vote, District resident Muriel Fritz draws attention to the continued struggle faced by all Washingtonians.

A SOUVENIR

of the

INAUGURATION

of a

President
of the United States
from Whose Election
Half-a-Million
American Citizens
Were Barred by
Constitutional
Disfranchisement

Above: Program passed out to attendees of President Herbert Hoover's inauguration in 1929. The pamphlet was designed to illustrate to those who attended the event that over half a million people were barred from voting in the election of Hoover, despite being United States citizens. Inside, Frederic Wile rewrote the words to "My Country 'Tis of Thee" to reflect the mood of many Washingtonians. A verse reads: "My District 'tis of thee, Land without liberty, Of thee I sing. Where Nation's laws are made, where income tax is paid, Yet, when all's done and said, Freedom can't ring."

Following pages: A group of Native Americans joined with members of the Vote for the District delegation to stage a protest at the 1936 Democratic National Convention in Philadelphia, Pennsylvania.

Above: Members of the House District Committee are seen discussing the 1939 proposed plan to reorganize the district government. *Left to right*: Representatives Ambrose Kennedy (MD), Jack Nichols (OK), George Bates (MA) and Everett Dirksen (IL).

Opposite, top: Senator William King, chair of the Senate District Committee, and District Commissioner Melvin Hazen (seated), along with (standing, left to right) Commissioner George Allen, Commissioner David McCoach Jr., Daniel Donovan and Elwood Seal. The August 1939 meeting, held at the District Building, was to review several proposed District reorganization proposals before King's Senate Committee.

Opposite, bottom: General view of the crowd gathered at the November 1939 District reorganization hearing in the board room of the District Building. Dr. George Havenner, of the Northwest Council, is shown speaking before the hearing.

District of Columbia Suffrage Association

BOND BUILDING, WASHINGTON, D. C.

Telephone REpublic 3431

Notice of Meeting

UNITED STATES CHAMBER OF COMMERCE BUILDING

Wednesday, June 21, 1939

A special meeting of the District of Columbia Suffrage Association will be held in the Auditorium of the U. S. Chamber of Commerce Building, Connecticut Ave. and H St., N. W., on Wednesday, June 21, 1939, at 8 o'clock p. m.

This meeting is held to give YOU a chance to say what YOU think of the recent developments in our city government, especially in view of the helpless condition of Washington residents, and in view of the arbitrary attitude of the Congress in denying them the right to be heard. The Association wants to know if YOU are satisfied to live under a **DICTATORSHIP**. This is an open meeting. **YOU** may talk about taxes, milk, asphalt, public welfare conditions, or anything concerning the present District of Columbia government.

To be sure that you have an opportunity to be heard, write or 'phone Suffrage headquarters and have your name on the list of those first to be recognized. NO PERSON MAY SPEAK MORE THAN FOUR MINUTES.

Above: View of the crowd at the hearing before the House District Committee discussing the proposed reorganization plan for the District of Columbia government. In the foreground are, *left to right*: Commissioner David McCoach Jr.; H.C. Whitehurst, director of highways; and Corporation Counsel Elwood Seal. The meeting took place in March 1939 at the House Office Building committee room.

Left: Following the passage of the Nineteenth Amendment, the District of Columbia Suffrage Association, originally chartered to help women gain the right to vote, focused its attention on the voting rights of all District residents. At this June 1939 meeting of the association, residents were given the opportunity to speak out about the proposed reorganization plan for the District and their feelings about living under the "dictatorship" of Congress.

The Early Days of the Home Rule Movement

Above: Several prominent civic leaders await their opportunity to testify before the House Reorganization Subcommittee in 1940. *From left to right*: John Saul, Board of Trade; Herbert Willett, Community Chest; Edgar Morris, Board of Trade; T.J. Spaulding; Arthur Sundlin, Merchants' and Manufacturers' Association; General Albert Cox, commander of the District National Guard; James Colliflower, Board of Trade; and Gardner Moore, Washington Hotel Association.

Below: Harry Wender, president of the Federation of Citizens Associations, is seen asking a question during the Senate District Committee hearing on the McCarran Home Rule Bill in December 1943. Members seen seated at the table include Dr. Meyer Jacobstein, Senator Harold Burton (OH) and Senator Patrick McCarran (NV).

The Early Days of the Home Rule Movement

It's in the bag!

Above: In December 1947, the members of the District of Columbia Suffrage Committee were once again hopeful that Santa would bring home rule to District residents for Christmas. Their hope was pinned to the Auchincloss Plan, which once again proposed home rule for the vote-less residents of the District. In a holiday flier, citizens were encouraged to "nudge" their congressman by telling him to vote for the plan, which only gave the right to vote for city officials, because it was a "good idea."

Opposite, top: Wilbur Finch, chairman of the District of Columbia Suffrage Committee, and former presidents of the Federation of Citizens Association Kenneth Armstrong and Harry Stull are seen at the Senate District Committee hearing on the McCarran Home Rule Bill in 1943.

Opposite, bottom: Wilbur Finch (left), chair of the District of Columbia Suffrage Committee, is seen speaking with Senator Patrick McCarran of Nevada during a Senate District Committee hearing in 1943. The committee heard testimony on the McCarran Home Rule Bill.

Above: In 1946, men dressed as founding fathers acted out a scene in which the Declaration of Independence was amended to guarantee the District a voice in national affairs. The participants were (from left to right) James Beattie, Jesse Ott, R. Cary Nichols Jr. and Coleman Diamond. Standing behind the men are Senators William Stanfill of Kentucky and Arthur Capper of Kansas.

Opposite, top: As in 1938, the D.C. League of Women Voters held plebiscites on the issue of voting rights throughout the District. Workers are seen here in 1946 posting the voting results at the District Building on election evening. These special voting events were held, in part, to illustrate to Congress that Washingtonians did indeed support voting rights and desired home rule.

Opposite, bottom: In 1946, citizens went to the polls to vote on the pending congressional suffrage legislation. Seen here (left to right) are F.C. Daniel, election judge and McKinley High School principal; Martin DeBroske; Walter Reich; H.J. Hooter; and Mrs. Hooter, who is casting her ballot.

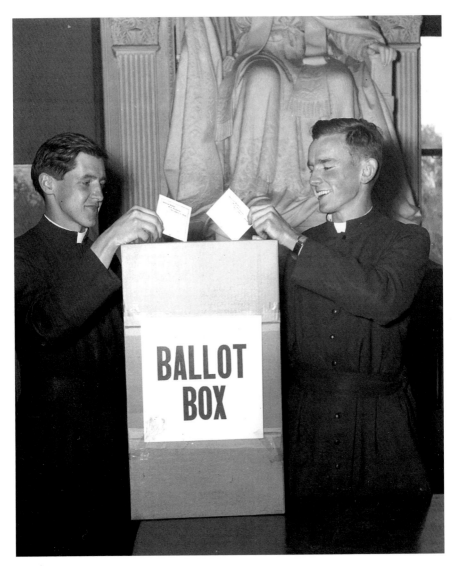

Brother Daniel Kennedy and Brother Joseph Fandel of the Order of Oblates of Mary Immaculate, students at Catholic University, are seen casting their ballots in the 1946 plebiscite.

Getting the facts about

HOME RULE

Answers to statements
made by opponents to
the Auchincloss Bill
with factual evidence
gathered and presented
by the Washington
Home Rule Committee.

MAY 3, 1948

Sub-committee on Publications:
CHARLES GLOVER III, SAMUEL SPENCER, MARSHALL HORNBLOWER, STURGIS WARNER

Above: Mrs. Willa Parker of the League of Women Shoppers is seen here collecting signatures on a petition urging Congress to table the District sales tax measure. The D.C. Women's Anti-Tax Committee sponsored the petition and led a fight to stop Congress from taxing the vote-less citizens of Washington. Mrs. Emmett Markwood, accompanied by her daughters Erica (left) and Valerie (right), take time to sign the petition while shopping downtown in 1947.

Left: Following the overwhelming support shown in the1946 plebiscites, D.C. suffrage groups like the Washington Home Rule Committee began publishing informational fliers. This 1948 work not only illustrates Washingtonians' support for home rule but also quotes a national poll that shows 77 percent of Americans in favor of D.C.'s right to vote.

At a February 1948 hearing in the old caucus room at the House Office Building, Senator Joseph Ball of Minnesota and Representative James Auchincloss of New Jersey listen to the testimony of Commissioner J. Russell Young.

"Miss Voteless District of Columbia," Anne Chodoff, pauses in front of the White House to draw attention to the plight of all Washingtonians. The 1952 demonstration, on the eve of Election Day, was staged by the District League of Women Voters.

The Early Days of the Home Rule Movement

Members of the Washington Chapter of the American Veterans Committee are seen doing an Indian war dance on the steps of the Senate Office Building in 1948. They staged what they called a "Potomac Tea Party" to show their opposition to the proposed 2 percent District of Columbia sales tax legislation. While on Capitol Hill, they presented members of Congress with tea bags bearing the slogan "taxation without representation is tyranny."

Mrs. Alice Bartlett, representing the Federation of Citizens Associations, signs the 1952 District Reorganization petition. The appeal, which shows support for the reorganization of the District government, was then sent to President Harry Truman. Looking on are (left to right) Mrs. C.D. Wright, District Federation of Women's Clubs; C.D. Merrill, Washington Board of Trade; Woolsey Hall, Federation of Civic Associations; and Martin Cook, veterans' organizations.

The Early Days of the Home Rule Movement

Above: Postal worker Frank Davis casts his ballot in the Democratic primaries at the firehouse located at Thirteenth and K Streets NW. Mr. Davis voted for Estes Kefauver because of his "stand on home rule." As a result of high voter turnout, Congress established the D.C. Board of Elections to carry out any future elections, and the District took one step closer to achieving home rule.

Opposite, top: At the stroke of midnight on July 1, 1952, Engineer Commissioner Bernard Robinson and Commissioners F. Joseph Donohue and Renah Camalier are shown signing the orders for the reorganization of the District government. Reorganization Plan No. 5 transferred to the three commissioners the functions of more than fifty boards.

Opposite, bottom: District residents wait in long lines to register to vote in the 1952 primary. Voters would be choosing delegates to the 1952 Democratic National Convention. The act of voting and the election of delegates was a very attractive means to show Congress that Washingtonians were indeed interested in the elective process and greatly desired home rule for themselves.

Election workers at the District Building are seen counting the ballots from the 1952 primary election only hours after the polls closed. Ballots were publicly counted by volunteers and members of the Democratic Central Committee. The election drew substantial voter turnout and large amounts of praise from other members of the electorate.

Following the success of the primary voting, Washingtonians took to the street in protest. Residents are seen here in 1954 staging a torchlight parade on the National Mall demanding the right to vote.

The Early Days of the Home Rule Movement

Left: At the District Building, residents line up to register to vote in the May 1, 1956 primary election. Registration was aided by the Junior Chamber of Commerce, which held a voter registration campaign that featured the attractive Miss Tippy Stringer playing the role of "Miss Get Out the Vote."

Below: Members of the District of Columbia Home Rule Committee, Senators Clifford Case (NJ), Patrick McNamara (MI), Matthew Neely (NJ) and Alan Bible (NV), are seen here talking outside the committee hearing chamber at the Capitol in 1955.

The Early Days of the Home Rule Movement

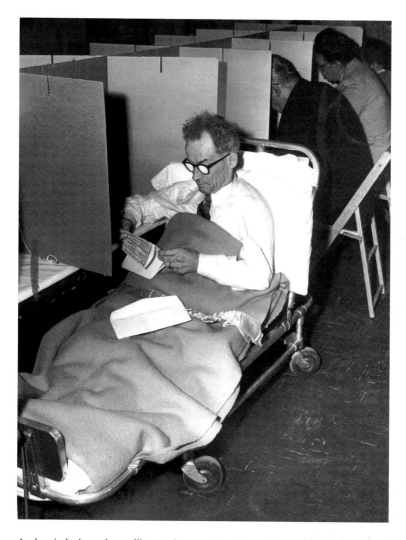

Above: At the city's sixty-nine polling stations, residents turned out to vote in great numbers to choose representation at the 1956 Democratic and Republican National Conventions. Joseph Evans, a patient at Doctors Hospital, was brought to the John Young Playground polling station in an ambulance and voted from the comfort of his portable cot.

Opposite, top: In 1956, Washingtonians once again went to the polls to elect delegates to the Democratic and Republican National Conventions and several other party officials. Here, Laura Morgan assists Dorothy Gassaway vote in the primary. Mrs. Gassaway was picked up and taken to the polls by a Democratic worker and was permitted to vote in the car since she was unable to walk into the polling location.

Opposite, bottom: Voters are seen here casting their ballots in the 1956 primary at the Mount Pleasant branch of the D.C. Public Library. Despite continued high voter turnout and national support in favor of giving the District the vote, southern segregationist congressmen continued to block any congressional home rule bills.

Above: A group of Washingtonians visiting the White House in 1957 presented President Dwight Eisenhower with a commemorative gift. Shown here are (left to right) Philip Brown, Board of Directors, Home Rule Committee; Mrs. Henry Munroe, League of Women Voters; Mrs. Harvey Moore, League of Women Voters; Commissioner David Karrick; and President Eisenhower.

Left: Dressed in colonial attire, these District residents make their support of D.C. home rule very clear. In 1959, Congressman Roy Wier of Minnesota introduced HR 1379, which called for Congress to "provide an elected mayor, city council, school board, and a non-voting delegate to the House of Representatives."

"Aloha"

Reprinted from WASHINGTON POST and TIMES HERALD
of March 13, 1959

In this 1959 Herbert Block, commonly known as "Herblock," cartoon "Aloha," the
United States Congress is shown laying out the welcome mat for the newly admitted state
of Hawaii over top of the "Voteless District of Columbia." With admittance into the
union, Hawaiians gained a voice in national policy making, while the plight of the District
residents continued to be ignored.

With the introduction of their Home Rule Bill in 1959, Congressmen William Widnall and Peter Frelinghuysen, both of New Jersey, symbolically struck off the "fetters" worn by Miss Carol Sharpe and Mrs. Chloeann Beck. The two women were picketing near the Capitol in a demonstration sponsored by the Washington Home Rule Committee.

THE HOME RULE CARTOONS
OF CLIFFORD BERRYMAN

C lifford K. Berryman is one of Washington, D.C.'s best-known political cartoonists of the twentieth century. Born in 1869 to James and Sallie Berryman, the tenth of eleven children, he spent his childhood in Versailles, Kentucky. He attended Professor Henry's School for Boys and graduated in 1886. At the age of thirteen, having no formal art training, he sketched a portrait of his idol, Congressman C.S. Blackburn. Blackburn happened to see the drawing and was so impressed that he sponsored Berryman's relocation to Washington, D.C., and procured him a position as a draftsman at the United States Patent Office.

In 1891, Berryman became the understudy to *Washington Post* cartoonist George Coffin. After Coffin's death in 1896, Berryman became the *Post*'s leading cartoonist. He was hired by the *Washington Star*, which had the largest circulation at the time, in 1907, and he continued to draw there until his death in 1949. Berryman satirized both sides of the political aisle. He is perhaps best known for the little bear featured in the 1902 *Post* cartoon entitled "Drawing the Line in Mississippi." The cartoon featured President Theodore Roosevelt refusing to kill a young bear cub because, as the story goes, the cub did not have a chance to defend itself. The iconic image of the bear stayed with the president and gave Morris and Rose Michtom the inspiration to create the first "teddy bear." In 1944, Berryman won the Pulitzer Prize for editorial cartooning for "But Where Is the Boat Going," which depicted President Roosevelt and other political leaders each trying to steer the "USS Manpower Mobilization" in opposite directions. These cartoons feature the colonial-clad character of "D.C.," whom Berryman created to represent the District of Columbia. "D.C." is frequently burdened with the ball and chain of "taxation without representation." Berryman often used occasions of national holidays such as Flag Day, the Fourth of July and Election Day to comment on the District's lack of representation.

Opposite, top: D.C. writes a letter to his "son," who is a part of the American Occupation Force stationed in Germany following the armistice that ended World War I. He notes that the Germans have voted in free elections and that the troops must feel a great satisfaction "enforcing the right of all people to vote." D.C. then notes that he misses them here at home, where not every citizen has the right to vote.

Opposite, bottom: A disheartened D.C. is comforted by the spirit of Abraham Lincoln, the Great Emancipator, after the Senate Judiciary Committee once again postponed a vote on the Sumners-Capper Amendment. Proposed by Hatton Sumners and Arthur Capper, the potential amendment to the Constitution would have granted voting rights to all Washingtonians; however, it became locked in committee and never reached the floor of the House of Representatives.

INDEPENDENCE DAY 1929.

A STUDY IN CONTRASTS

The Home Rule Cartoons of Clifford Berryman

Above: A proud Uncle Sam looks on as a large group of congressmen attempts to board the "Votes for the District" wagon being driven by D.C. Already onboard are Hatton Sumners (TX), Jennings Randolph (WV), Samuel Rayburn (TX), William Bankhead (AL), Ambrose Kennedy (RI) and Joseph W. Martin Jr. (MA). Willkie is seen attempting to climb into the wagon.

Opposite, top: A young D.C. attempts to buy fireworks to celebrate the Fourth of July; however, Uncle Sam refuses to sell him the larger "Independence" firecrackers. Instead, he forces D.C. to take and be satisfied with the silent "voteless sparklers."

Opposite, bottom: In "A Study in Contrasts," Uncle Sam welcomes a throng of naturalized citizens to America on "I Am an American Day" and bestows full voting rights upon them. Meanwhile, a shackled and cold D.C. looks on in disbelief.

Above: D.C., carrying a placard in one hand and his ball and chain in the other, marches with renewed enthusiasm as he gleefully reminds voters to take part in the plebiscite on November 5. Uncle Sam and Teddy, Berryman's famous bear, look on with amazement and wonder why all voters don't have this much spirit when it comes to voting.

Opposite, top: A disgusted D.C., standing behind an iron fence, watches as other citizens head to the polls to cast their votes on Election Day. He holds a sign that says "half a million disfranchised citizens."

Opposite, bottom: In "Geographical Note," Berryman notes that "the Potomac River isolates the American Capital from American Principles." D.C. is shown wearing his ball and chain, standing on the eastern bank of the Potomac River looking at the large crowd of Virginians heading to the polls in Arlington County. With a sense of irony, Berryman places the slogan "The Citizen's Duty is to Vote" above the polling room door.

Geographical Note: The Potomac River Isolates the American Capital from American Principles.

FLAG DAY, 1933

The Home Rule Cartoons of Clifford Berryman

Above: Here, D.C. is seen holding a forty-eight-starred American flag in one hand and in the other a star with the slogan "D.C. National Representation." Even in the earliest days of the fight for home rule, some suggested that the District be granted statehood. However, this movement did not gain full momentum until the early 1980s.

Opposite, top: For Flag Day in 1933, Berryman shows D.C. longingly looking at the American flag, stating that it is "a beautiful emblem and a joy to look upon but it means taxation without representation to me."

Opposite, bottom: On the 157th anniversary of the Boston Tea Party, D.C. is shown pointing at several boxes of "taxation without representation tea" and stating that it is "long since overtime to throw this overboard." The plight of the vote-less District of Columbia has long been connected to the Tea Party thrown by colonials in Boston in 1773 to oppose a new royal tax on tea imports. Washingtonians feel that they are "in the same boat" with the colonials, even going so far as to adopt their slogan, "taxation with representation."

PAUL REVERE OF 1933.

COLUMBUS DAY 1932

The Home Rule Cartoons of Clifford Berryman

INDEPENDENCE DAY, 1932

Above: On Independence Day 1932, D.C. is shown celebrating with his vote-less sparklers, while those states with smaller populations celebrate with "suffrage skyrockets" and "representation fireworks." According to the 1930 census, 488,000 persons lived in the District of Columbia and there were eight states that had smaller populations. They were New Hampshire, Idaho, Arizona, New Mexico, Vermont, Delaware, Wyoming and Nevada.

Opposite, top: A long 158 years after Paul Revere made his historic ride in Boston, Berryman shows D.C. riding past the Forty-second Congress of the Daughters of the American Revolution, taking place at Constitution Hall, shouting, "Join in the fight here against taxation without representation."

Opposite, bottom: For the 1932 Columbus Day cartoon, Berryman shows D.C. in the "no vote" stockades, while Christopher Columbus questions Uncle Sam by asking, "After 440 years isn't he old enough to vote?" Teddy is seen clutching Uncle Sam's leg.

The Home Rule Cartoons of Clifford Berryman

Above: The "young democrat," dressed in colonial attire, speaks to D.C. in disbelief as he points to a picture of the Boston Tea Party and states, "You're still taxed but not represented." D.C., sitting at the desk, is looking over the two latest home rule bills suggested by Congress, HRJ 169 and SJ 9.

Opposite, top: D.C. is seen sitting at a desk while Uncle Sam presents him with a list of things he will not forget, including their part in paying taxes, volunteering soldiers for defense and an "obedience to law enforcement." D.C.'s simple response is, "Yeah but you forgot me on Election Day."

Opposite, bottom: On Election Day, Uncle Sam tells D.C. as he attempts to cast his vote that he needs to "go way back and sit down." In the background is a chair labeled "1773, no taxation without representation"; however, the word "no" has been crossed out. The date is the year of the Boston Tea Party and the Revolution-era slogan has been altered to reflect that District residents do indeed pay federal taxes but still do not have any form of representation. Teddy can be seen in the background shamefully covering his eyes and holding a sign that says "what our forefathers fought for."

WASHINGTON, D.C. PROTESTS

Above: Teddy sounds a bugle call while Uncle Sam proclaims that all must go to their polling places to register with the Selective Service. D.C., pointing out that he has no polling place, says that he will be there "all the same." Passed in 1940, the Selective Training and Service Act established the first peacetime conscription in U.S. history. It required all males between the ages of eighteen and sixty-five to register for Selective Service.

Opposite, top: On the anniversary of the Boston Tea Party, D.C. stands at his desk proclaiming that "if women put on war paint District representation will come with a rush." On the desk are various papers listing the names of national organizations that support the District's fight for home rule and voting rights. Among the groups that support D.C. are the National League of Women Voters, American Federation of Teachers and the National Council of Jewish Women.

Opposite, bottom: D.C., surrounded by papers representing various federal taxes paid by Washingtonians, looks at a painting entitled the *Beginning of the War Against Taxation Without Representation, April 19, 1775*, and states that he believes "that war was never won." On that date, the first military action of the American Revolution happened in the Massachusetts towns of Lexington and Concord with the shot heard 'round the world.

The Home Rule Cartoons of Clifford Berryman

On the 163rd anniversary of the Boston Tea Party, D.C. is seen floating in the water moments after he has been thrown overboard by the sailor "Congress" aboard the ship *U.S.* Still on the deck of the ship are several boxes, labeled "taxation without representation," and D.C. remarks to the sailor that those were supposed to go overboard, not him.

For the 165th anniversary of the Boston Tea Party, President Franklin Roosevelt is shown as captain of the *Good Ship Democracy*. D.C. asks him to throw the large "taxation without representation" box overboard because it is "poison to democracy."

DEMONSTRATING FOR
CIVIL RIGHTS

Historians have long dated the start of the modern civil rights movement with the 1954 landmark case *Brown v. Board of Education*. This decision unanimously overturned the "separate but equal" era created by the *Plessy v. Ferguson* ruling in 1896. In the Washington, D.C. area, the fight for equality might be traced to Irene Morgan. In 1944, she boarded a Greyhound bus in Gloucester County, Virginia, bound for Baltimore, Maryland. Seated in the "colored" section, she refused to move when a white couple boarded and needed the seats. The driver stopped in Middlesex County and summoned the local sheriff to arrest Morgan. She tore up the warrant and kicked the sheriff in the groin as she was being forcibly removed from the bus. She was charged with resisting arrest and violating Virginia's segregation law. She pled guilty to the first charge and paid a $1,000 fine. On the latter charge, she pled not guilty, but the judge found her guilty and fined her $10, which she refused to pay. After losing several appeals, she appealed her case to the United States Supreme Court on the grounds that it violated the Interstate Commerce clause of the U.S. Constitution. Morgan stated, "If something happens to you which is wrong, the best thing to do is have it corrected in the best way you can, the best thing for me to do was to go to the Supreme Court." In a 7–1, ruling the Supreme Court agreed with Morgan and ruled that the Virginia enforcement of segregation laws on interstate buses was illegal.

This action might not have sparked the national attention that Rosa Parks's deed did, but it does illustrate this area's growing unrest with unequal civil liberties. Little by little, the Jim Crow era was coming to an end as people began to challenge the status quo. From lynching laws to employment issues, Washingtonians have always taken to the streets in protest. If the early days of the modern civil rights movement taught Washingtonians one important lesson, it would be that there was power in numbers.

Opposite, top: View of a civil rights parade at the corner of Eleventh and Vermont Avenues NW. Marchers are urging Capitol Transit to employ Negro drivers. As the war in Europe was escalating and more men went off to fight for their country, the public transit system faced a critical shortage of able drivers, and civil right leaders saw this as an opportunity to gain equal access to employment opportunities for the black community.

Opposite, bottom: Marchers heading toward Franklin Park, at Thirteenth and K Streets NW, are not only showing their support for the war effort and the defeat of the Axis powers, but they are also seeking increased employment opportunities for black workers. The 1943 march was designed to push Capitol Transit toward giving black employees the opportunity to work for the transportation company during this war-induced manpower shortage.

Demonstrating for Civil Rights

Above: Like those officials seeking home rule for the District, civil rights leaders in 1944 sought to effect change through a legislative means. Here, three black leaders are seen following their meeting with President Franklin Roosevelt, who pledged his support for their civil rights concerns. *From left to right*: Walter White, NAACP; Mary McLeod Bethune, National Council of Negro Women; and Channing Tobias, Universities' Mission to Central Africa.

Left: During the early days of the post–World War II era, civil rights support came from many different places. Here, members of the Washington Branch of the Workers Party equate the fight against Jim Crow as "support" for the party's Socialist agenda.

Demonstrating for Civil Rights

Members of the Washington Committee of the Southern Conference for Human Welfare are shown here picketing the Fisher Auditorium on the campus of George Washington University in 1946. They were picketing against the theatre's decision to bar blacks from the opening of a new play starring Ingrid Bergman. The small-scale demonstrations were organized following Bergman's statement that she would not have come to the capital if she had known that blacks were going to be barred from the theatre.

Above: Members of the Washington Branch of the Workers Party are seen lending their support for the civil rights movement through their opposition to Jim Crow. While many different groups with different national agendas lent their support during the early phases of the civil rights movement, it was not until the "modern era" that the national leadership began to focus its efforts on key social issues.

Left: Following the *Morgan v. Virginia* ruling in 1946, Virginia was forced to desegregate all interstate buses. Here, James Thomas of Washington is seen boarding a bus bound for Virginia at the terminal located at Twelfth Street and Pennsylvania Avenue. The newspaper he is holding explains it all.

A driver for the Arnold Bus Line is seen here taking down the race segregation signs onboard his bus before he begins his run into Virginia. In 1946, the Supreme Court ruled that the segregation of interstate transportation violated the Interstate Commerce clause of the U.S. Constitution and was therefore unconstitutional.

In 1947, President Harry Truman becomes the first president to address the National Association for the Advancement of Colored People. He spoke to the group from the steps of the Lincoln Memorial, saying that "there is no justifiable reason for discrimination because of ancestry, religion, race, or color."

Captain Covelle of the Metropolitan Police Department speaks with members of the Civil Rights Congress as they march past police headquarters in the District. The demonstrators are carrying a coffin labeled "don't bury American freedom" and are protesting what they call the "stormtroopering" tactics of some police officers.

Local members of the National Association of Colored Women are seen here picketing in front of the White House (circa 1950). They are asking the president to publicly speak out against the practice of lynching in the South.

Demonstrating for Civil Rights

Picketers outside the White House in 1951 are asking President Harry Truman to stop the scheduled execution of the seven Martinsville, Virginia black men who were convicted of raping a white woman. These picketers believe that the civil rights of the convicted men were violated when they were tried by an all-white jury. Truman refused to grant clemency, and in February 1951 the men were all executed. In 1977, the Supreme Court ruled that the crime of rape could not be punishable by death. The plight of the Martinsville Seven helped to change federal rape laws.

Spotswood Thomas Bolling Jr. and his mother, Sarah, embrace following the Supreme Court's ruling in 1954 that ended segregation in the D.C. public school system. Four years earlier, Bolling and ten other students were refused entry into John Philips Sousa Junior High School based on their race. Howard University professor James Nabrit filed suit on their behalf. After the District Court dismissed the case, the Supreme Court granted "writ of certiorari" to the case. The justices ruled that the students were indeed deprived their right to due process under the protection of the Fifth Amendment, because racial segregation in the schools constituted an arbitrary deprivation of their liberty.

Following the *Bolling v. Sharpe* ruling by the Supreme Court, which ended segregation in the D.C. public school system, Mrs. Ella Rice became one of the first black teachers hired by the school system. She was assigned to Henry Draper Elementary School, where she taught for a number of years.

On May 17, 1957, a three-hour rally, called the Prayer Pilgrimage for Freedom, took place at the Lincoln Memorial. A host of speakers orated on several different civil rights themes, but it was a young Martin Luther King Jr. who captured the national attention. Making his first national speech, King spoke on a topic that was near and dear to all Washingtonians. The speech was called "Give Us the Ballot." Here, King, A. Philip Randolph and Roy Wilkins are seen receiving the key to the city from Commissioner Robert McLaughlin following the conclusion of the rally.

TWENTY-THIRD AMENDMENT

When the District of Columbia was established in 1801, the founding fathers had to believe that the city would only be a center of government and not a population center. One hundred years later, the population was over 250,000, and by the 1950s the number of people calling Washington, D.C., home had tripled. With three quarters of a million people now calling D.C. home, it seemed odd that people living in twelve states with smaller populations had more voting rights than District residents. By constitutional law, voting in presidential elections was a right reserved only for states, and since the District was not a state, no vote for president was ever conducted.

In August 1959, the Senate Subcommittee on Constitutional Amendments opened hearing on two resolutions. The first, proposed by Senator Spessard Holland of Florida, was an anti–poll tax amendment that never made it out of committee. The second concerned national representation for citizens of the District of Columbia. It was proposed by Senators Francis Case of South Dakota, James Beall of Maryland and Kenneth Keating of New York. After months of debate, Tennessee senator Estes Kefauver opened a September hearing by stating that there was "no reason under the sun why District residents should not have the vote." After months of continued debate over representation in the Electoral College, a final version was agreed upon, and on June 17, 1960, Congress passed the Twenty-third Amendment bill. Six days later, Hawaii became the first state to ratify it, and 285 days later Ohio's ratification gave the required three-fourths majority needed.

It is important to note that this amendment does not make the District a state; it simply confers upon its citizens the number of electors that it would have if it were indeed a state. The amendment does not provide full representation in Congress or even provide for self-government; that would have to wait. However, for a city that had endured more than 150 years without a federal vote, any change was good. The 1964 presidential election witnessed nearly 200,000 votes being cast. The city supported the ticket of Lyndon Johnson and Hubert Humphrey, who won 85 percent of the votes.

Opposite, top: Velma Koontz (seated), Ruth Miller and W. Herbert Gill, members of the Citizens for Presidential Vote, review some documents at their office as they await news on the ratification of the Twenty-third Amendment.

Opposite, bottom: Velma Koontz used her lipstick to write "victory" across her calendar. On March 29, 1961, 285 days after Hawaii became the first to approve, the State of Ohio ratified the amendment, thus giving it the two-thirds majority needed to become law.

Twenty-third Amendment

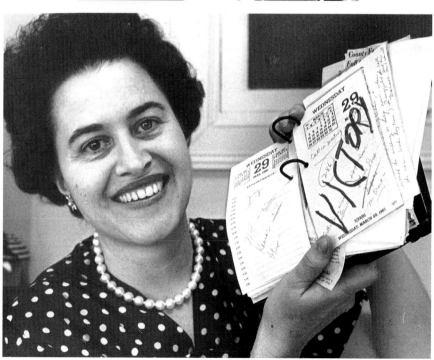

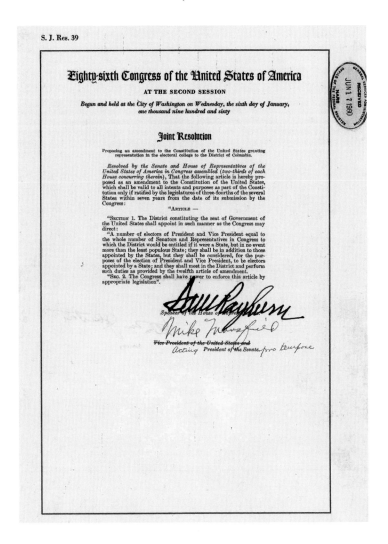

Above: A copy of the proposed amendment to the Constitution presented to the states by the Eighty-sixth Congress for ratification on January 6, 1960. The document is signed by Speaker of the House Samuel Rayburn (TX) and Acting President of the Senate Mike Mansfield (MT).

Opposite, top: As the states debated over ratification in 1960, *Washington Post* cartoonist Herbert Block, commonly known as "Herblock," drew this political cartoon entitled "It Hardly Seems Possible." The District of Columbia is shown as having been stranded on the "without a vote for any public office" island for the past eighty-seven years. Off in the distance, the ship *23rd Amendment*, with its three electoral votes, sails to his rescue.

Opposite, bottom: In this cartoon by the *Washington Star*'s Gibson Crockett, D.C. is shown celebrating a National Vote. With the passage of the Twenty-third Amendment, Washingtonians finally had something to celebrate, and as the title of the cartoon suggests, it was the "Fourth of July in June."

Above: Civil rights leader and longtime District resident Joseph Rauh leads happy members of the Democratic Central Committee as they march down Fourteenth Street toward the District Building. Once there, the marchers registered to vote in the first meaningful election in generations.

Left: In 1964, District residents began to register to vote for the first time in a generation. Here, at the District Building, voters line up to register to vote in the upcoming presidential election.

Left: Leading the "Get Out to Register" parade in February 1964 are Yvonne Brock, Yolanda Wade and Deborah Powell. The parade was sponsored by the Mount Olivet Junior Citizens Association.

Below: Annie Brown takes the oath administered by registrar Mrs. John Allen prior to registering to vote. This common ceremony, underwent by all who registered, was conducted at the 73rd precinct located at John Tyler Elementary School, Tenth and G Streets SE.

Above: On May 5, 1964, voters arrived early to vote in the District of Columbia primary. Seen here are voters heading to the polls at the Chevy Chase Community Center on Connecticut Avenue NW. Republican Committee members were there to assist those who had not yet registered to vote in the November election.

Opposite, top: Members of the League of Women Voters, dressed in the attire of suffragettes from fifty years ago, toured downtown Washington in this horse-drawn carriage urging Washingtonians to register to vote. The coachman is Charlotte Price, head of the Leagues Speakers' Bureau. Seated in the rear of the carriage are Nettie Ottenberg, a founder of the D.C. chapter of the League, and Jane Hammer, the vice-president of the League in 1964.

Opposite, bottom: In the Board of Elections at the District Building, Chairman Charles Mayer holds the hat containing the name capsules while Delores Woods draws the names. The drawing was to determine the placement on the 1964 primary ballot. Woods selected the name Dedmon from the hat.

For the first time in his life, ninety-seven-year-old John Harry, a lifelong resident of the District of Columbia, casts his ballot in November 1964. He and his son Edward cast their ballots at Janney Elementary School on Albemarle Street NW.

Twenty-third Amendment

Left: Following the November 1964 election night activities, sealed ballot boxes were sent to the Board of Elections office in the District Building. Here, Dan Noll, secretary of the Board of Elections, is seen inspecting the boxes shortly after their arrival.

Below: University of Maryland senior Joe Hoffman, along with Catholic University students Mike Mague Jr., Bob Burke and Frank Byron, is seen counting ballots at the D.C. Armory following the primary election in May 1964. They were among the hundreds of volunteers who helped make D.C.'s first-ever presidential election a resounding success.

The 1960s and the Push for Civil Rights

With the *Brown v. Board of Education* decision in 1954, the approach of the civil rights movement shifted from public education, legislative lobbying and litigation to a more direct line of action. Boycotts, sit-ins, freedom rides and marches were now adopted by the movement's leadership. These tactics relied on the mobilization of large numbers of people and the philosophy of nonviolent resistance and civil disobedience. Churches, as the centers of communities, and hundreds of local organizations mobilized volunteers in large numbers. This more direct form of resistance captivated the media spotlight and helped to facilitate the rapid change that traditional court-mounted challenges could not duplicate. Over the next decade, events such as the Montgomery Bus Boycott, Mississippi Freedom Summer, Selma and the March on Washington became beacons of change. This radical shift to nonviolent resistance forced the federal government to react with several key pieces of legislation: the Civil Rights Act of 1964, which banned discrimination in employment and public accommodations; the Voting Rights Act of 1965, which restored and protected the rights given in the Fifteenth Amendment; and the Civil Rights Act of 1968, which banned discrimination in rental and housing sales. With increased devotion to a cause, African Americans reentered the political arena and pushed for increased acceptance. They have continued to show that "the time," as Dr. Martin Luther King Jr. said, "is always right to do what is right."

During this era, Washingtonians learned firsthand how to garner national attention for issues of civil rights. The District's greatest civil rights challenge has always been its desire for home rule. Leaders in the community adopted the methods and actions of this new approach to demonstrating for civil rights. With a strong grass-roots campaign based in neighborhood organizations and the church, Washingtonians were able to push the home rule agenda to center stage and gather national attention for their continued fight.

Opposite, top: One of the most integral parts of the nonviolent strategy during the civil rights movement was the implementation of the sit-in. Widely employed by Mahatma Gandhi in the fight for Indian independence, the sit-in was used very effectively by civil rights demonstrators. On June 9, 1960, these "sit-inners" are seen patiently waiting for services at a lunch counter in Arlington, Virginia. Rather than serve a black patron, the manager of this counter decided to close for the day.

Opposite, bottom: Perhaps the most famous sit-in in American history happened at a Woolworth's lunch counter in Greensboro, North Carolina. Following this event, a wave of anti-segregation sit-ins occurred throughout the country. Here, Montgomery County detectives are seen reading arrest warrants to the sit-in participants at a restaurant counter in Rockville, Maryland. Following their arrest on July 10, 1960, these demonstrators were taken to the courthouse for arraignment.

Following pages: One of the hallmarks of the modern era of the civil rights movement was mass demonstrations. Here, marchers descend on the District Building, spilling over into Freedom Plaza. Attacking the racial problems through legislative means only brought the movement so far; however, the injection of large nonviolent demonstrations and marches enabled the movement to attract a greater audience and enact faster change.

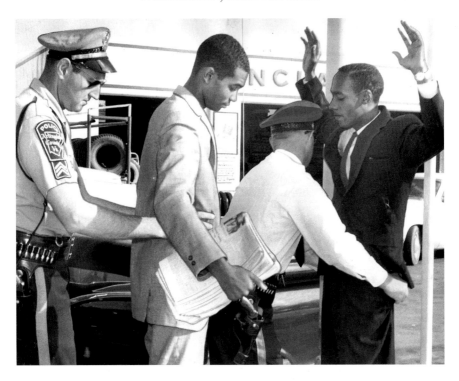

Above: Arlington County Police Sergeant Roy Lokey and Lieutenant Ernest Summers search two black men arrested for staging a sit-in at the local Howard Johnson's restaurant. Dion Diamond and Laurence Henry were charged with trespassing and taken to police headquarters on June 11, 1960.

Opposite, top: Although the landmark case of *Brown v. Board of Education* did away with the "separate but equal" era in America, it did not extend that equality to the workplace. Here, local ministers are seen picketing some of the banks along Fifteenth Street NW near the White House in 1961. Their message was simple: let a black man work in jobs other than those that were seen as being in a "menial capacity."

Opposite, bottom: After finishing their demonstration at a nearby bank, where they voiced their opinions about hiring practices at some banks, these local religious leaders stop in front of the White House for a moment of prayer. The 1961 demonstration included, among others, the Reverend R.H. Baddy, Reverend E. Franklin Jackson, Reverend S.E. Guiles and Reverend James Foy.

Above: Following his remarks, the Reverend Smallwood Williams, bishop of the Bible Way Church of Our Lord Jesus Christ Worldwide, Inc., offers a prayer in front of the White House during the 1963 Rally Against Racial Discrimination. At the extreme right is the Reverend E. Franklin Jackson, president of the D.C. branch of the National Association for the Advancement of Colored People.

Opposite, top: Marchers assemble in Lafayette Park for the 1963 Rally Against Racial Discrimination. Some of the leaders of this march are seen here. Holding the "S.C.L.C. wants freedom now" sign is Reverend Walter Fauntroy, and to the left are Reverend Smallwood Williams and Reverend E. Franklin Jackson. To the right of Fauntroy are Congressman Charles Diggs Jr. (MI) and C. Sumner Stone.

Opposite, bottom: In Lafayette Park, across from the White House, marchers at the 1963 Rally Against Racial Discrimination listen to the remarks of the Reverend Smallwood Williams, director of activities for the Southern Christian Leadership Conference. He is surrounded by many local and national civil rights leaders.

Marchers at the 1963 Rally Against Racial Discrimination gather at the Department of Justice building, where they demanded to hear from Attorney General Bobby Kennedy. Marchers voiced their disappointment with the Kennedy administration's lack of progress in ending racial discrimination in the job market.

Only a handful of marchers, most of them children, were in the Washington contingent of the Congress of Racial Equality at the 1963 Rally Against Racial Discrimination. Marchers are seen here starting out from Eighteenth and H Streets NW and heading to the main rally in Lafayette Park.

Washington Congress of Racial Equality marchers are seen here listening to a speech by an unidentified person during the 1963 Rally Against Racial Discrimination. This small group of local marchers joined with the larger group of marchers in Lafayette Park before heading toward the District Building and the Department of Justice on Pennsylvania Avenue.

The 1960s and the Push for Civil Rights

Attorney General Robert Kennedy, using a portable loudspeaker, addresses a portion of the crowd of some three thousand marchers who participated in the 1963 Rally Against Racial Discrimination. Kennedy told the group of civil rights demonstrators that the present administration has done much to wipe out racial discrimination, "but there is still a long way to go."

Reverend Walter Fauntroy addresses the media at a July 11, 1963 press conference on the planned August civil rights demonstration. The march was organized by a group of civil rights, labor and religious leaders under the theme of "jobs and freedom" and is estimated to be the largest civil rights demonstration in American history. Fauntroy, joined by Police Chief Robert Murray and other leaders, served as the march coordinator.

The 1963 March on Washington for Jobs and Freedom was the idea of A. Philip Randolph, who had proposed a similar march in 1941. The 1963 march was organized by Randolph, James Farmer, John Lewis, Roy Wilkins, Whitney Young, Bayard Rustin and Martin Luther King Jr. Pictured here is the banner raised by march officials to designate the headquarters tent. According to one reporter, the National Mall took on a carnival-like appearance, covered with informational booths, first aid stations and other conveniences for the marchers.

Volunteers worked into the night assembling signs to be carried by the marchers. Here, workers in the storage room at radio station WUST on the corner of Ninth and V Streets NW display some of the signs to be used at the March on Washington.

The 1960s and the Push for Civil Rights

College students Nancy Couturie and Mike Cunningham are among the hundreds of volunteers who helped make the March on Washington such a success. On a tent on the National Mall, thousands of additional placards were assembled.

On the eve of the March on Washington, the marshals' tent became the center of all activities. During the next day's events, all aspects of the march were controlled and directed from this tent, which was erected on the National Mall near the Washington Monument.

The 1960s and the Push for Civil Rights

Above: An estimated 300,000 people attended the March on Washington for Jobs and Freedom; marchers are seen here heading down Constitution Avenue on their way to the Lincoln Memorial. The march is widely credited with helping to pass the Civil Rights Act of 1964 and the National Voting Rights Act of 1965. A massive amount of media attention was given to the march; in fact, there were more cameras used on that day than covered the last presidential inauguration. The movement and its leaders enjoyed an unprecedented level of exposure. From this event, local leaders gained valuable connections in Congress and in the media that would soon help them as they became more aggressive in their quest for home rule in the District.

Opposite, top: On the morning of August 28, 1963, pre-dawn prayer services were held at a number of local churches. Here, residents and visitors raise their voices in prayer at the Bible Way Church located at 1130 New Jersey Avenue NW. At the peak of the modern civil rights movement, the church became a powerful organizer, with its leaders often taking very active roles in the movement.

Oppoite, bottom: The District not only provided leadership and volunteer labor for the March on Washington, but an outpouring of Washingtonians also flooded the Ellipse just south of the White House, waiting for their chance to join the procession to the Lincoln Memorial. Many came directly from early morning church services, and all bore placards urging improvements in civil rights, while others took the opportunity to put in a plug for the District's struggle for home rule. An estimated twenty-five thousand residents participated in the march.

The 1960s and the Push for Civil Rights

Above: Aerial view of Lafayette Park during the September 23, 1963 march in memorial of the four black girls killed in Birmingham, Alabama. Their death inspired songs, poems, novels and even an Oscar-winning documentary, but perhaps the greatest legacy of this tragic event was the passage of the Civil Rights Act of 1964.

Opposite, top: The September 23, 1963 march in memory of the Birmingham church bombing victims was organized by the Washington chapter of the Congress of Racial Equality and featured marchers carrying banners that read "no more Birminghams." Marchers, including Julius Hobson (center), are seen singing "We Shall Overcome" in Lafayette Park at the conclusion of the march.

Opposite, bottom: Crowds gathered at All Souls Unitarian Church, Sixteenth and Harvard Streets NW, on September 23, 1963. Local civil rights leaders organized a memorial service and march for the four black girls killed in the recent racially motivated church bombing in Birmingham, Alabama. Marchers are seen here gathering outside the church following the service as they prepare to march down Sixteenth Street toward the White House.

The 1960s and the Push for Civil Rights

Above: The Right Reverend Monsignor George Gingras and Reverend Walter Fauntroy were among the speakers at a March 14, 1965 rally in Lafayette Park to support civil rights demonstrators in Selma, Alabama. After the brutal attacks on peaceful marches on the day better known as "Bloody Sunday," protesters almost immediately began showing up at the White House, demanding that federal troops be sent to protect the marchers.

Opposite, top: Nancy Duncan, a student at Georgetown University, is the first speaker in the weeklong Student Filibuster for Civil Rights. The event, held the week of April 27, 1964, at the Sylvan Theater on the Washington Monument grounds, featured local college students speaking continuously from 10:00 a.m. to 8:00 p.m. for five days. Their hope was to encourage the Senate to pass the civil rights act currently before it. The Civil Rights Act of 1964 languished in the Senate for fifty-seven days, being blocked by the "Southern Bloc" and several filibusters. Finally, a weaker compromise bill was passed and enacted into law on July 2, 1964.

Opposite, bottom: The man in the center wearing the hat is Richard Brown of Washington, D.C. He is seen here speaking with reporters outside the White House in 1965, where Brown had just staged a sit-in. His reasons were simple: it was "because there has been no action in Selma." Selma, Alabama, had been refusing to allow blacks to register to vote following months of demonstrations, arrests and violence. The actions in Selma concluded with the Selma to Montgomery March of 1965.

The 1960s and the Push for Civil Rights

Above: On March, 12, 1967, the Reverend Martin Luther King Jr., seen here with his son Marty and Reverend Walter Fauntroy, led a ten-block parade through the Shaw area of Washington. King was here to show his support and rally the citizens behind the planned urban renewal in their neighborhood. He stated that he "believes that you on these 675 acres called Shaw can point the way for the nation out of her most serious domestic dilemma—the decay of the city."

Opposite, top: A group representing Associated Community Teams (ACT) pickets the White House Conference on Negro Rights taking place at the Sheraton Park Hotel in June 1966. Its members are concerned that blacks do not receive equal justice in the District of Columbia courts. Incidents of racial profiling and false arrests in the Watts section of Los Angeles led to six days of riots that left 34 people dead, 1,032 injured and 3,952 arrested, and 977 buildings destroyed.

Opposite, bottom: Joseph Randolph, William Smith and James Banks are seen here waiting to board a train at Union Station bound for Mississippi. They are just a few of the local civil rights campaigners heading to Jackson, Mississippi, to be part of James Meredith's March Against Fear, which took place in June 1966.

During the National Anthem, students at the Eastern vs. Spingarn football game on October 18, 1968, gave the Black Power arm raise. First used by Howard University professor Stokely Carmichael in 1966 as a social and political term, "Black Power" expresses a wide range of political goals and ideologies. The raised fist salute was made famous at the 1968 Summer Olympics by Tommie Smith and John Carlos. Historically, the salute has been regarded as an expression of solidarity, strength or defiance.

A group of thirty-five protestors, calling themselves the Young Committee for Equal Justice, staged a sit-in at the office of Commissioner Walter Tobriner on May 17, 1967. The protestors were upset that the District commissioners had decided not to open a special committee to probe the fatal shooting of a Northeast youth in a struggle with police.

DEMANDING THE VOICE
OF HOME RULE

I f there was one thing that Washingtonians took from their experiences in the civil rights movement, it was how to mobilize and rally people to a cause. From their involvement, D.C. leaders formed bonds with many prominent civil rights leaders. Perhaps the single most important bond was that between the Reverend Walter Fauntroy and Dr. Martin Luther King Jr. The two men first met when Fauntroy was attending Virginia Union University, and they became good friends following an all-night discussion on the subject of theology. Fauntroy joined King's Southern Christian Leadership Conference and became the director of the Washington Bureau. It was in this capacity that Fauntroy emerged as an influential lobbyist for civil rights in Congress. Fauntroy was also selected by King to help coordinate the seminal 1963 March on Washington for Jobs and Freedom. From working with King, Fauntroy made many political connections in D.C., including a personal relationship with President Lyndon Johnson.

In 1965, King showed his support for D.C. home rule by attending a small march and rally organized by Fauntroy. In Lafayette Square, King stated that Congress had been "derelict in their duties and sacred responsibility to make justice and freedom a reality for all citizens of the District of Columbia." On July 17, 1966, another large rally was held in support of home rule. The four-hour Home Rule Day gathering, held on the grounds of the Washington Monument, brought together thirty-two speakers who repeatedly sounded the theme of coalition. They urged all District residents, black and white, that they must work together to achieve the goal of home rule. Fauntroy said that given the right to vote, "we will give the nation and the world a much needed example of how Negroes and whites can work together."

Despite the continued pressure and growing support for the movement, Congress still failed to address the desire of many Washingtonians, as another legislative session came to a close. As the 200th anniversary of the Boston Tea Party approached, a small group of Washingtonians staged its own reenactment in 1973. As Congress debated the Home Rule Act, a wheelchair-bound Julius Hobson spoke to the crowd. "This is the 100th time I've been to a home rule rally…it's not a tea party—it's a revolution that's going to be needed to get home rule." Hobson's harsh words illustrated the growing apathy and frustration among those who had been struggling for decades. Eight months later, Congress passed the Home Rule Act.

Members of the District Democratic Committee rode this nineteenth-century stagecoach around the streets of Washington in 1965 to draw attention to a "Dollars for Home Rule Now" drive. Committee members William Porter and Helen Leavitt occupy the rear seats.

Demanding the Voice of Home Rule

Above: Float riders, at the inauguration of President Johnson in 1965, included Miss USA and former Miss District of Columbia Bobbie Johnson. Seen here at the start of the parade, the District's demands for the newly sworn-in president were very clear. Johnson responded to this outcry by sending a special message to Congress on February 2, 1965, that began: "The restoration of home rule to the citizens of the District of Columbia must no longer be delayed."

Opposite, top: Representative Fred Schwengel of Iowa is seen here addressing a group of home rule supporters at a November 14, 1963 meeting at All Souls Unitarian Church. The crowd of over eight hundred people listened to a parade of legislators, clergymen, labor and civil rights leaders speak on the need for home rule. Schwengel told the crowd that the main reason why he asked to be assigned to the House District Committee was so he could help eliminate the need for a District Committee by getting home rule for all Washingtonians.

Opposite, bottom: At the January 20, 1965 parade following the inauguration of President Lyndon Johnson, the District of Columbia sponsored a float that delivered a very clear message. With the passage of the Twenty-third Amendment, District citizens voiced their support for President Johnson. Washingtonians now looked to Johnson, a friend to the District's struggle for home rule in Congress, to help complete the journey to self-government.

Above: Supporters of the Free D.C. movement marched along H Street NE on March 12, 1966, to celebrate the merchants who proudly displayed "Free D.C." stickers in their windows. The movement was organized by Marion Berry and encouraged residents to only shop at area businesses that supported the home rule movement. In 1966, Berry boasted that more than 350 stores in the Northeast section had already joined the movement. However, support for the movement faded after the NAACP withdrew its support following a change in policy that included economic boycotts.

Opposite, top: In August 1965, Reverend Martin Luther King Jr., along with local civil rights and home rule leaders, led a march of about 5,000 persons from the playground at Eleventh and R Streets NW to Lafayette Square. King vowed to lead 200,000 marchers in Washington if the city was not given home rule "in the next few weeks."

Opposite, bottom: Reverend Martin Luther King Jr., Reverend Walter Fauntroy, Right Reverend Paul Moore Jr., Walter Abernathy and Reverend Andrew Young were among the estimated five thousand marchers who descended on Lafayette Park on August 5, 1965. The purpose of the march was not only to show the deep feelings for home rule but also to thank President Lyndon Johnson for strongly supporting the home rule bill currently before Congress.

Dick Gregory (middle), comedian and civil rights activist, leads a group of Southwest residents to the site of the Home Rule Day rally on the National Mall. The 1966 rally was sponsored by the Youth Organizations United for Home Rule in D.C. and drew an estimated four thousand people.

A view of the crowd seated on the grass at the Sylvan Theater on the grounds of the Washington Monument for the 1966 Home Rule Day rally, which featured thirty-two speakers. Many of the speakers called for a broadly based coalition of support that would hopefully be able to rally 80 to 90 percent of Washingtonians to the home rule movement.

Above: View of the stage during the opening remarks and playing of the National Anthem at the July 17, 1966 Home Rule Day rally. Eugene Kinlow, an official in the Youth Organizations United for Home Rule in D.C., read a proclamation from the District commissioners designating the day as "Home Rule Day" in the District of Columbia.

Left: Comedian and civil rights activist Dick Gregory, who flew in from riot-torn Chicago, addressed the crowd with a series of jokes and anecdotes before reminding the audience that "you can't laugh your problems away." He went on to note that it was indeed "frightening" that bricks had become the only language that those in power seemed to understand.

Left: As home rule supporters rallied on the National Mall near the Washington Monument in 1966, Congress was once again debating the issue inside the Capitol. The legislation at hand sought to bring a measure of home rule to Washingtonians by allowing for the elected city school board. Despite growing support in the community, legislators were locked in a squabble over an antipoverty bill, and the home rule measure failed to make it out of committee hearings.

Below: Senator Jacob Javits of New York is seen here speaking to the crowd at the 1966 Home Rule Day rally. Javits pledged his support for a home rule rider attached to Senator Wayne Morse's higher education bill. He said that the passage of this home rule legislation was an "opportunity to strike a blow for human dignity which we cannot afford to reject."

Young supporters of home rule for the District show their support at the 1966 Home Rule Day rally. Four thousand people attended the rally, listening to thirty-two speakers pledging their support for District home rule. Midway through the rally, Marion Berry, leader of the Free D.C. Movement, arrived and stood outside the fenced-in area. Berry, who was asked to speak at the rally but declined the offer, seemed disappointed with the turnout, saying that "with all that muscle they should have had 20 times the people."

Sign painter Herbert Parham is seen here creating placards for the 1966 Home Rule Day rally. For whatever donation marchers could afford to give, Parham created signs and posters for them to carry during the parade and rally.

Demanding the Voice of Home Rule

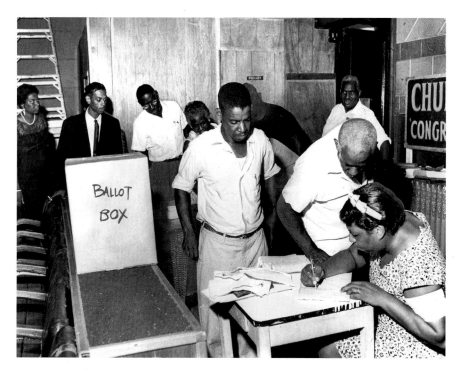

District of Columbia citizens in the Shaw area took to the polls in a "mock vote" held on August 20, 1967. More than one thousand people came to the old Raphael Theater to vote for candidates for the new city council. Names of the winning candidates were sent to President Lyndon Johnson, who would be selecting the newly formed nine-member council.

Many organizations conducted informal straw votes for prospective nominees for leadership posts in the city's new, reorganized government. The Washington Committee on Black Power mounted the largest and sent ten "Votemobiles," like this one with Julius Hobson in the right seat, traveling throughout the District.

WASHINGTON, D.C. PROTESTS

Above: Members of the American Federation of Teachers demonstrate in support of home rule in 1967 near First Street and Maryland Avenue. Executive Order No. 11379, signed by President Lyndon Johnson on November 8, 1967, did away with the three-commissioner system and replaced it with an appointed mayor and city council.

Opposite, top: In 1967, President Lyndon Johnson convinced Congress to finally do away with the three-commissioner form of government. It was replaced with a presidentially appointed mayor-commissioner and a nine-member city council. This was the scene as Walter Washington was being sworn in at the White House on September 28, 1967. *Left to right*: Margerie Fletcher, Bennetta Washington, Deputy Mayor Thomas Fletcher, Supreme Court justice Abe Fortas, Mayor Walter Washington (taking oath), Lady Bird Johnson and President Lyndon Johnson.

Opposite, bottom: On November 7, 1967, Mayor Walter Washington is seen here at the District Building addressing the first meeting of the new District City Council. The nine-member council consisted of (from left to right) Stanley Anderson, Margaret Haywood, John Nevius, Walter Fauntroy, John Hechinger, Polly Shackleton, William Thompson, J.C. Turner and Joseph Yeidell.

Demanding the Voice of Home Rule

Top: In 1970, members of the District of Columbia chapter of the League of Women Voters marched in support of home rule and the District's plight of "taxation without representation." The marchers, led by chapter president Mrs. Philip Fortune (center), are seen crossing Pennsylvania Avenue on their way to the District Building. The league was conducting a nationwide petition drive to support the D.C. home rule movement.

Bottom: Marchers at the April 1970 League of Women Voters parade, many of them carrying "taxation without representation" signs, are seen crossing Pennsylvania Avenue at Thirteenth Street near the District Building. Since February, League members had been collecting signatures on a home rule petition to be sent to Congress. A week of activities was planned to promote the event, and the League hoped to gather 1.5 million signatures.

Young marchers are seen here participating in the 1970 League of Women Voters parade. Mayor Walter Washington proclaimed the week of April 15 as "Petition Week," as churches, civic groups and League members actively gathered signatures on a home rule petition to be sent to Congress. Other events included a concert and a "mourning" club meeting in the lobby of the Longworth Building.

The 1773 Boston Tea Party was perpetrated because Bostonians were upset by the Crown's decision to impose a tax on the importation of tea. Colonists were forced to accept this and other taxes without an opportunity to oppose them in Parliament. This marcher at the 1970 League of Women Voters parade shows her disappointment with the District's colonial status in Congress by displaying tea bags on her umbrella.

Demanding the Voice of Home Rule

Above: A spectator at the 1972 home rule hearing at the Capitol shows her displeasure with Congress's treatment of Washingtonians. For over 170 years, Washington, D.C., has been denied any political voice in the halls of Congress and its residents have been unfairly taxed and underrepresented; Washingtonians have long been pushing for full representation. Some believe that with the victories of the 1960s and '70s the fight for home rule is over; however, until the District has full representation in Congress and complete home rule, the fight will continue.

Opposite, top: Invoking the spirit of the Boston Tea Party, this marcher at the League of Women Voters parade in 1970 is seen showing her support for the District's home rule by hanging "taxation without representation" tea bags from her umbrella.

Opposite, bottom: In 1973, in commemoration of the 200th anniversary of the Boston Tea Party, Washingtonians displayed their displeasure with Congress and President Richard Nixon's lack of support for providing District representation in the House of Representatives. The group, called Self Determination for D.C., stages the mock Tea Party and is seen here throwing "tea" crates into the Potomac River.

CITY ELECTIONS

Soon after President Lyndon Johnson took office, he began openly supporting the District's right to home rule. Having been a well-respected congressman, Johnson was able to use his influence to discharge home rule legislation from hostile committees and support the failed Multer Bill, which provided for an elected mayor and council and a non-voting delegate to the House of Representatives. Using the Reorganization Act of 1949, which gave the president power to reorganize executive branch government agencies provided that Congress did not disapprove within sixty days, Johnson submitted a plan to congress on June 1, 1967. This plan placed all responsibility and authority in a single commissioner, who would have a deputy commissioner to assist him. Additionally, the plan provided for a nine-member council to be empowered with some legislative functions. The Senate passed the measure after three days of hearings, while the House of Representatives took almost the entire sixty days to debate the issue. When the final vote was taken on August 11, 1967, 160 members rejected the plan and 244 members approved; Johnson wasted little time in nominating persons to fill the new positions. Walter Washington was appointed as commissioner and Thomas Fletcher was made the assistant to the commissioner. The members of the first council were John Hechinger, Walter Fauntroy, Margaret Haywood, J.C. Turner, Joseph Yeldell, John Nevius, Stanley Anderson, William Thompson and Polly Shackleton.

Since Johnson's reorganization plan, Congress began to slowly give Washingtonians increased voting rights on local issues. The first came in

1968, when Congress granted citizens the right to elect their own members to the Public School Board of Education. It was in this election that a young Marion Barry first emerged on the political scene. Congress then approved the District of Columbia Election Act in 1970, which gave citizens the authority to elect a non-voting delegate to the House of Representatives. Walter Fauntroy was sworn in on March 23, 1971, as the first delegate to represent the citizens of the District of Columbia. Although the non-voting delegate is not allowed a floor vote, he is permitted a committee vote and is able it introduce legislation on any issue.

In 1973, Congress passed perhaps the single most important piece of legislation in the 172-year struggle for home rule. The District of Columbia Self-Government and Governmental Reorganization Act, or Home Rule Charter, was signed into law by President Richard Nixon. The law provides for an elected mayor and a thirteen-member council. Other provisions included the creation of a federal enclave, congressional control of the city's budget and the creation of advisory neighborhood councils. The charter was overwhelmingly supported by district votes in a special election held on May 7, 1974. Although the Home Rule Charter does not grant the District complete home rule, it has provided a noticeably enhanced voice to city electors in the control of local affairs.

In May 1970, the League of Women Voters presented copies of its petition, complete with 1.2 million signatures, to members of Congress. The member is seen here showing her support for the District gaining the right to vote in Congress. At this time, the House District Committee was considering a bill already passed by the Senate that would give Washingtonians a non-voting delegate to the House of Representatives.

Above: Prior to the 1970 special election, where for the first time in nearly one hundred years Washingtonians would have the chance to elect a representative to Congress, District Board of Election worker Novall Perkins is seen inspecting one of the ballot boxes to be used in the November election.

Opposite, top: These children from Takoma Park Elementary School are waiting to see Congressman Carl Perkins of Kentucky. In 1970, the students' teacher, Janet Moss, involved them to take part in a classroom discussion on the District's need for home rule. When asked by a staff member why they wanted home rule, the children responded, "All the states have home rule and we're like a state…we're taxed without representation."

Opposite, bottom: With the passage of the District of Columbia Election Act of 1970, Washingtonians were given the right to elect a non-voting delegate to Congress. Here, the Reverend Walter Fauntroy is seen campaigning with Coretta Scott King and Clifford Alexander along Twelfth Street NW.

Above: After voting in the March 1971 special election, volunteers are seen here counting ballots at the Pensions Building, now the National Building Museum. Walter Fauntroy received 58 percent of the vote, beating his nearest competitor by nearly forty thousand votes.

Opposite, top: Reverend Walter Fauntroy is seen here in 1971 flashing the "V" sign to his supporters at the Hamilton Hotel following the news of his victory in the race for non-voting delegate to the House of Representatives. He stated that "it was an exhilarating experience in learning the ways of politics, in being Americans for the first time."

Opposite, bottom: On April 19, 1971, Walter Fauntroy was sworn in as the first non-voting delegate to the House of Representatives. Fauntroy served as the District's representative until 1991, when he was replaced by our current representative, Eleanor Holmes Norton. In the 1980s, Fauntroy led the charge for a constitutional amendment to give the district full voting power in both the Senate and the House.

With the election of a representative to Congress, Washingtonians now turned their attention to having the ability to freely elect their own mayor and city council. Local preparatory school students show their support for home rule at the District Building during a 1973 rally.

Members of the D.C. chapter of the Urban League raise their hands in a show of unity at an October 1973 home rule rally at the District Building. Washingtonians were dismayed when it was learned that President Richard Nixon, who had publicly proclaimed his support for home rule, had begun to work on several fronts to privately oppose the latest home rule measure.

Mayor Walter Washington speaking to the crowd gathered at the District Building for the 1973 home rule rally. He told the crowd of nearly four hundred people that home rule was "a cause whose time has come. Why is it that we have to prove we're ready for self-determination?…Just give us what we are entitled to."

Katharine Gresham spends her fourth night volunteering with Common Cause, contacting congressional districts in an attempt to drum up support for D.C. home rule. In 1973, Congress became deadlocked on the issue of home rule once again. The bill before Congress would allow for the election of all city officials; however, it was the provisions in the bill that defined Congress's power over District action that had members locked in debate.

Above: Before the home rule meeting in 1974, this woman studies the fact sheet on the recently passed D.C. Home Rule Act. On December 24, 1973, Congress passed the District of Columbia Home Rule Act, which provided for a freely elected mayor, a twelve-member city council and the establishment of Advisory Neighborhood Councils.

Left: The new Home Rule Charter was to be voted on by the citizens of the District of Columbia in a special election set for May 7, 1974. At meetings held throughout the city, District residents questioned the provisions and studied the facts about home rule. Perhaps the most glaring provision was that Congress still had veto power over any new District laws and that the city's budget was still controlled by Congress.

City Elections

Sterling Tucker, Jerry Moore and Congressman Don Fraser of Minnesota discuss the Home Rule Charter with residents of Ward 4 at a meeting on April, 24, 1974. Citizens voting on the May referendum still had many unanswered questions, even as the May 7 voting day approached.

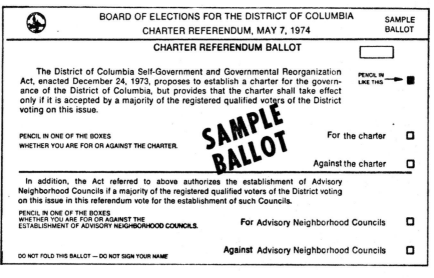

BOARD OF ELECTIONS FOR THE DISTRICT OF COLUMBIA

CHARTER REFERENDUM, MAY 7, 1974

SAMPLE BALLOT

CHARTER REFERENDUM BALLOT

The District of Columbia Self-Government and Governmental Reorganization Act, enacted December 24, 1973, proposes to establish a charter for the governance of the District of Columbia, but provides that the charter shall take effect only if it is accepted by a majority of the registered qualified voters of the District voting on this issue.

PENCIL IN LIKE THIS ➡ ■

PENCIL IN ONE OF THE BOXES
WHETHER YOU ARE FOR OR AGAINST THE CHARTER.

SAMPLE BALLOT

For the charter ☐

Against the charter ☐

In addition, the Act referred to above authorizes the establishment of Advisory Neighborhood Councils if a majority of the registered qualified voters of the District voting on this issue vote for the establishment of such Councils.

PENCIL IN ONE OF THE BOXES
WHETHER YOU ARE FOR OR AGAINST THE
ESTABLISHMENT OF ADVISORY NEIGHBORHOOD COUNCILS.

For Advisory Neighborhood Councils ☐

Against Advisory Neighborhood Councils ☐

DO NOT FOLD THIS BALLOT — DO NOT SIGN YOUR NAME

The ballot was simple to understand: for or against the Home Rule Charter and for or against the establishment of Neighborhood Advisory Councils. Despite the provisions that still gave Congress authority over some aspects of District politics, voters hungry for home rule widely supported the Home Rule Charter. In fact, a Georgetown University poll found that nearly 75 percent of those asked planned to vote for the charter.

Left: Many local organizations, with the reality of home rule in sight, began to push for voters to approve the Home Rule Charter during the May 7, 1974 special election. Gina Mosley, age three, is seen here urging residents to "use it" at a get out to vote rally at Hine Junior High School in Southeast.

Below: On Election Day, May 7, 1974, Mayor Walter Washington and his wife Bennetta receive their ballots from Earlene Williams. The mayor cast his ballot for home rule at Meyer Elementary School on the corner of Eleventh and Clifton Streets NW.

Left: Throughout the city, parades and rallies gathered support for the approval of the Home Rule Charter. At the Martin Luther King Jr. Memorial Library, librarian Teresia Hurd is seen here putting the finishing touches on the get out and vote display.

Below: Mayor Walter Washington and school board member Abe Rosenfield, at the Board of Elections headquarters, react happily as Home Rule Charter election results are posted. With over 40 percent voter turnout, Washingtonians overwhelmingly accepted the proposed Home Rule Charter, with 79,141 voting for and 16,518 against.

After seven years as the presidentially appointed mayor-commissioner, Walter Washington became the District's first elected mayor in over one hundred years. He is seen here on election night celebrating his election with his wife Bennetta at the Washington Hotel.

More than five hundred people crowded near the tent at the District Building on January 3, 1975, to witness Mayor Walter Washington and the thirteen city council members take their oaths of office. In his address, Mayor Washington recalled the steps toward home rule for all Washingtonians and racial equality for its black residents.

Bennetta Washington watches as Chief Justice Thurgood Marshall administers the oath of office to her husband on the steps of the District Building. Mayor Washington commented that in a time of increased inflation and curtailed federal spending, the attainment of home rule was like "taking over a bad neighborhood and getting blamed" for its terrible condition.

With limited home rule achieved, Washingtonians now turned their attention toward another problem: no voting representation in Congress. Delegate Walter Fauntroy in 1975 is seen holding up a bumper sticker that evokes the old theme of "taxation without representation" as the renewed political rallying cry. During his career in Congress, Fauntroy, like his current counterpart Eleanor Holms Norton, led many unsuccessful attempts to gain congressional voting rights for the District.

With only a paltry 13 percent of eligible Washingtonians actually voting in the 1978 primary and only two out of three voting in the presidential election, many groups who fought so hard for home rule now turned their attention to getting District residents to actually use the right they fought for. Marilyn Bryant, a volunteer with I Vote, displays new "shouldn't we vote" T-shirts. As its slogan went, "If you think voting will get you nothing, not voting will guarantee you nothing."

After four years in elected office, Walter Washington kicks off his reelection campaign at the Washington Hotel. Washington, having been labeled as an ineffective city manager, would lose the 1978 election to Marion Berry and become a partner in a New York-based law firm.

THE FIGHT CONTINUES

Since the Home Rule Charter of 1973, citizens of the District of Columbia have continued to push for complete and autonomous home rule. In 1978, the D.C. Voting Rights Amendment, which was proposed by Congressman Don Edwards of California, received overwhelming support from both houses of Congress. It was sent to the state legislatures but only received sixteen of the thirty-eight ratifications needed. In 1980, Washingtonians passed an initiative calling for a constitutional convention for a new state. Voters ratified the constitution for New Columbia in 1982, and since that time, legislation to enact this proposed state constitution has been routinely introduced in Congress, but none has ever passed. The statehood campaign stalled after the failure of the D.C. Voting Rights Amendment in 1985; however, a new constitution was drafted in 1987 and again was offered to Congress for ratification. The last serious push for statehood came in 1993, when the legislation was defeated in the House of Representatives by a vote of 277 to 153.

Since 1971, the D.C. Statehood Party, now known as the D.C. Statehood Green Party, has been the primary voice for District independence. In 1997, it was joined by the Stand Up For Democracy in D.C. Coalition, commonly referred to as Stand Up! or Free D.C.

In 2009, Congresswoman Eleanor Holmes Norton, D.C.'s current non-voting delegate, proposed the D.C. Voting Rights Act. For the first time, the measure passed the U.S. Senate, and it is currently under consideration by the House of Representatives. HR 157 would give full congressional voting rights to the District's representation in Congress; however, if the bill is passed and signed into law by the president, there are many who believe that it would not withstand a constitutional challenge in the Supreme Court. The main emphasis of these continued attempts in Congress is as it has always been: to bring attention to the plight of the citizens of the District of Columbia who have never been granted all the freedoms enjoyed by every other citizen in the United States. However, the question still remains: when will these rights finally be granted and who will be leading that charge?

In this 1972 cartoon by *Milwaukee Journal* cartoonist Bill Sanders, pandas at the National Zoo show how great it is "to be here in the land of democracy." Attached to a flier by the group Self-Determination for D.C., this cartoon was used to gain support for the home rule movement from persons outside the District of Columbia. Over fifty national organizations granted access to their mailing lists to organizations such as this in order for Washingtonians to rally support for their cause.

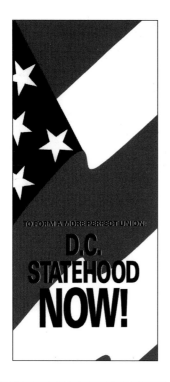

Top, left: In 1978, Washingtonians began efforts to ratify a proposed amendment to the Constitution that would provide full congressional voting rights; however, their efforts failed, as only a few states ratified the amendment. In 1980, District citizens voted in favor of a new initiative and formed the D.C. Statehood Commission.

Top, right: In 1982, delegates to the D.C. Statehood Commission completed work on the Constitution for the State of New Columbia. The constitution was adopted by the citizens of the District of Columbia by popular vote in November. The petition for statehood and the constitution were transmitted by Mayor Marion Berry to Congress in 1983.

Bottom: The campaign for statehood stalled as the D.C. Voting Rights Amendment failed to gain the required ratification in 1985. In 1987, a second constitution for New Columbia was drafted and again submitted to Congress, but it has failed to gain any support. The last serious debate on the issue of statehood occurred in 1993, when the measure was defeated in the House of Representatives by a vote of 277 to 153.

Distributed by the D.C. League of Women Voters in 1983, this pamphlet supports the ratification of the D.C. Voting Rights Amendment. Claiming that it was an "oversight" by the founding fathers, since they did not intend for people to live in the federal district, the League urged its national membership to actively support the amendment in their own state.

HOME RULE
FOR WASHINGTON, D. C.

Washingtonians have supported their country with taxes, given the lives of their young men and women in times of war and obeyed the law written for them. The thirteen colonies shared the idea of representation afforded new states thirty-seven different times. Simple justice demands that the fifty states now share it with their capital.

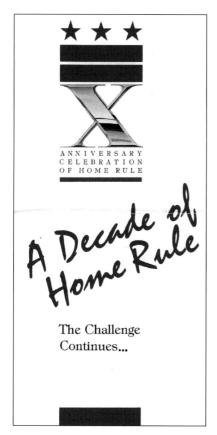

Left: In 1985, the District celebrated a decade of home rule with essay contests, galas, concerts and symposiums. Even as the D.C. Voting Rights Amendment failed to gain ratification, Washingtonians had a lot to celebrate. However, despite all this celebrating, many Washingtonians understood that there was still a lot of work to be done; after all, we still languish under taxation without representation.

Below: The League of Women Voters continued to be the District's biggest supporter of home rule; however, despite their support, Washingtonians have been unable to persuade Congress to give them a congressional vote.

Did you know that residents of the District of Columbia have no voting representation in Congress? With just one non-voting delegate, we still have taxation without representation.

As a holiday present to us, we'd appreciate it if you would ask your state legislators to ratify the D.C. Amendment to the U.S. Constitution. This will give those of us in D.C. the same voice in government that all other Americans have.

Published by
The League of Women Voters of the District of Columbia

FRIDAY, MARCH 30TH, 2001, 6:00 TO 9:00 PM

DC DEM✪CRACY SEVEN
C E L E B R A T I O N !

A T   T H E

T O U T O R S K Y   M A N S I O N

1 7 2 0   1 6 T H   S T R E E T ,   N W

In 1998, Congress effectively overturned a citizens' ballot initiative. With all avenues for redressing grievances about congressional voting representation blocked, including two Supreme Court cases, seven Washingtonians staged a demonstration at the Capitol in 2000 as Congress debated the District's budget. When a vote on the budget was called for, the Democracy Seven, as they became known, stood up and cast their votes in opposition.

This cartoon by Chris Bishop was created after the conclusion of the 2000 presidential election and the controversy over the Florida vote. Due to the closeness of the election, several recounts were ordered, each going to George W. Bush. The U.S. Supreme Court ordered any additional recounts be halted and certified the election results. With this ruling, many Floridians felt disenfranchised and thus formed a common bond with Washingtonians, who have long understood this plight.

In November 2000, the D.C. Department of Motor Vehicles began issuing license plates bearing the slogan "taxation without representation." In a show of support for the District's plight, President Bill Clinton had the plates placed on the presidential limousine. In 2002, the city council authorized the placement of the slogan on the district's flag; however, no new flag design has been approved.

At the District Building, the city council installed this message board to tally the federal taxes paid by Washingtonians since the beginning of 2009. Council chairman Vincent C. Gray stated that "the purpose of installing the 'tax-ticker'…was to draw attention to the fact that District residents pay the same federal taxes as all other American citizens, however, we do not have the same democratic representation in the United States Congress." *Image by Mark Greek.*

vAlthough there are visible signs of the continued fight for home rule and full voting representation sprinkled throughout the District, it may seem to some that the movement has stalled. This sign, sponsored by D.C. Vote, hangs above the entrance to RFK Stadium. The large-scale demonstrations have been replaced with aggressive lobbying and silent or individual protests, while a new generation of Washingtonians, born into the era of limited home rule, seems to be satisfied with the status quo. *Image by Christopher Copetas.*

About the Author

M ark Stephen Greek is the photo archivist for the District of Columbia Public Libraries, Washingtoniana Division, and has been working to preserve the images of the *Washington Star* photograph collection since 2002. With knowledge of the images pertaining to the events that helped shape the landscape of the District, Mark has compiled a collection of photographs that will help readers better understand the struggle that still continues today. Mark was born in Pittsburgh, Pennsylvania, and received his bachelor of arts in American history from the University of Pittsburgh and his masters of arts in American history from the University of South Carolina. He is a member of the Academy of Certified Archivists, the Society of American Archivists and the American Library Association and serves on the program committee for the Conference on Washington, D.C. Historical Studies.

Visit us at
www.historypress.net